TIGER OF THE SNOWS

ROBERT BURLEIGH AND ED YOUNG

Tenzing Norgay: The boy whose dream was Everest

TIGER OF THE SNOWS

Atheneum Books for Young Readers

New York London Toronto Sydney

A song for Tenzing,
Tenzing Norgay,
Sherpa,
Mountain man,
Tiger of the snows,
Because today
He will climb to the top of the world:
Everest,
Snow-plumed Chomolungma,
Mother Goddess of the Earth,
Sharpest tooth in the jaw of the great dragon,
Mountain so tall no bird can fly over it.
Twenty-nine thousand feet,
Five miles high.
Mountain,
Mother of the Winds, I hear your voice.

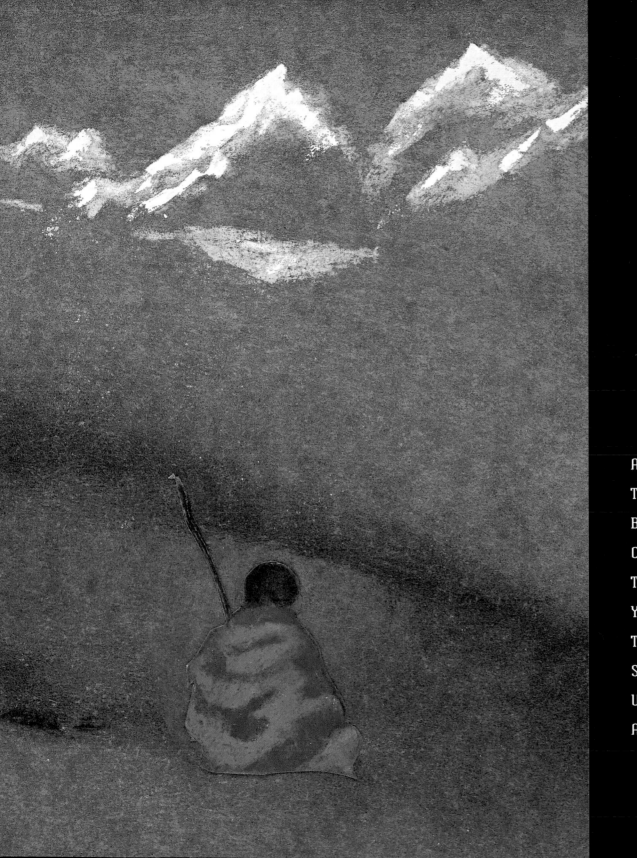

A song for Tenzing,

Tenzing Norgay,

Born to heights,

Child of the Himalayas,

Today the man,

Yesterday the boy on a steep hillside,

Tending the belled yaks,

Spring in his blood,

Wandering through patches of rhododend

And as ever, looking up:

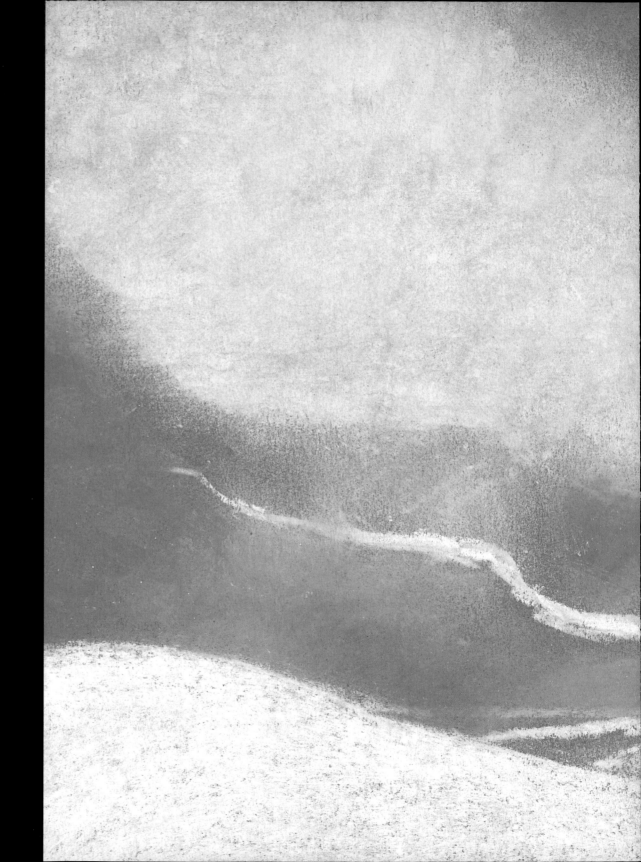

There, there,
The snow-dotted black-rock peak,
Sky's partner,
crown of whiteness swirling into the air,
Mountain of so many names,
His mountain.
Could he, little Tenzing,
Dream so far and so high?
Mountain,
Mountain,
Why do you call me?

A song for Tenzing,

Tenzing Norgay,

Pathfinder,

Hungry for the taste of clouds,

The young man Tenzing,

He who carried stones in his knapsack,

Who stole off to fabled Katmandu,

(City of chimes and statues),

Unlocked the secrets of the climber's rope,

Studied the lore of the axe,

And apprenticed himself to death and danger

Plunging crevasses,

Ice falls,

Blizzards,

Glaciers agleam with a green light,

The boom-sound of cascading snow.

Buried inside a bottomless blackness:

Where was up?

Ah, bright light! Here! Still alive!

Mountain,

Mountain,

I have made myself ready.

A song for Tenzing,

Tenzing Norgay,

Paver of the way,

Carver of steps to the impossible,

Because today,

May 29, 1953,

He will climb to the very top of the world.

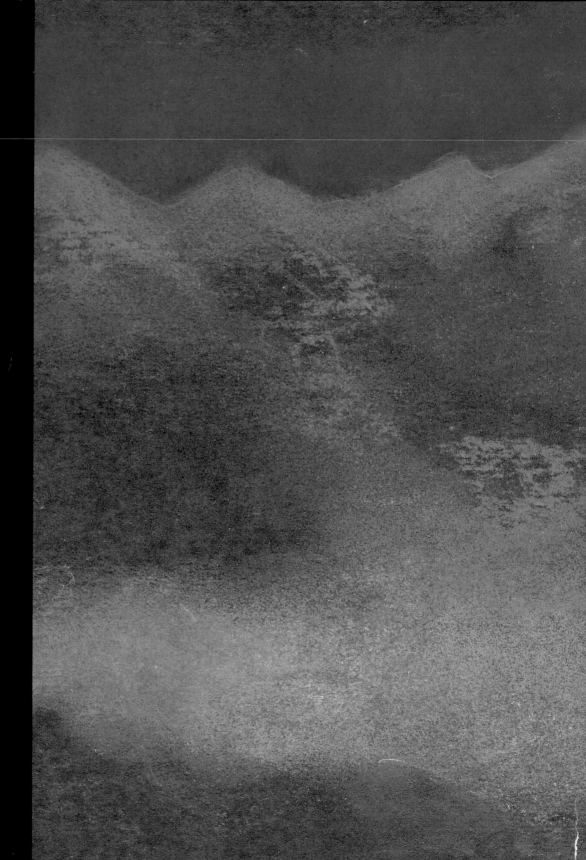

At dawn he stands on a narrow ledge,

Sights the valley that was once his home,

Sees the far-flung crests as calm as robed Buddhas,

Utters a silent prayer

For all those who came before,

And tried—and failed.

He calls softly to dark-goggled Edmund Hillary:

It is time.

Six thirty. Seventeen below.

Windless and clear.

(One thousand feet more.)

Mountain,

Mountain,

The wheel of my life is turning, turning.

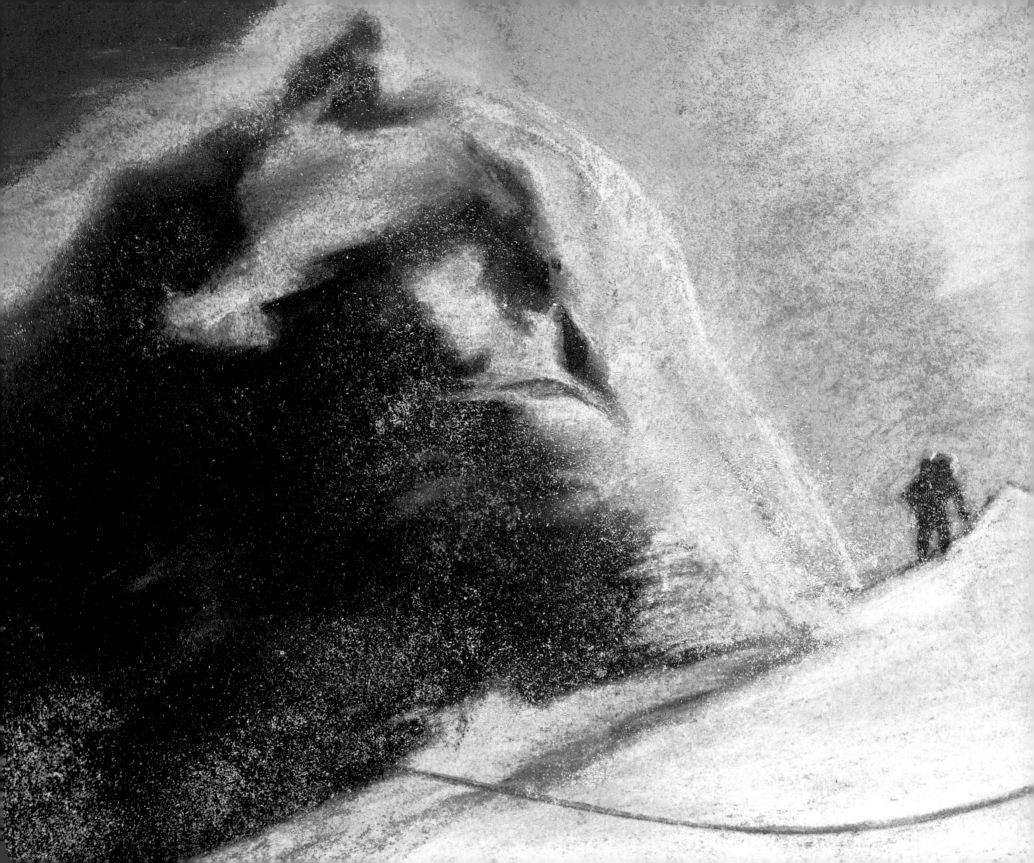

A song for Tenzing,

Tenzing Norgay,

Deep-lunged,

Quick-footed,

Climbing into the airles

Agile as a cat,

Into the Zone of Death.

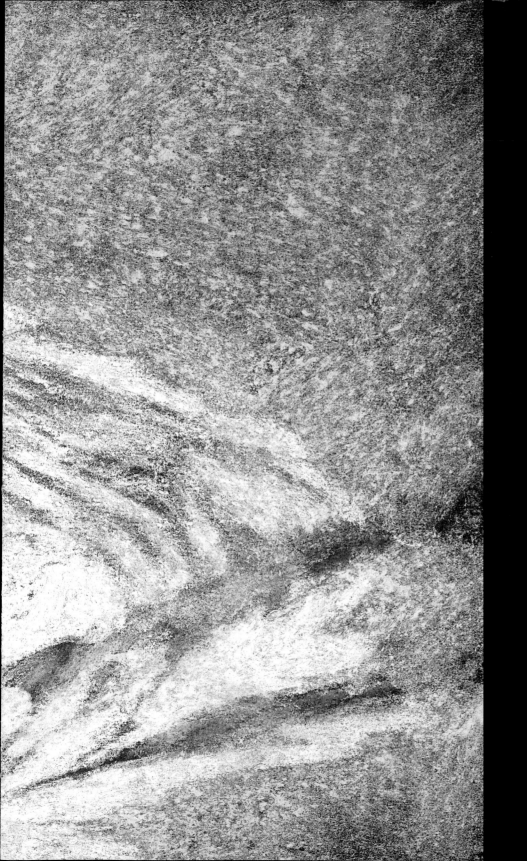

He hears the creak of shoulder straps and crunch of boots
Looks back on chasms of down-falling darkness,
Tugs and takes in slack.
Roped to Hillary, fellow climber,
He slips and slides,
Plunges the axe and holds fast,
Gulps oxygen, like a beached fish,
Strains forward on saddles of black ice,
Riding the white horse higher and higher,
Up and up and up
Between stone and frozen cornices.
Zest becomes struggle.
Arms are tree trunks,
Feet turn to chunks of lead,
Stumbling past mounds of wind-sculpted snow.

Suddenly,

The rise above them falls away.

Are we here?

See—an unbelievable vastness on every side!

Mountain,

Mountain,

I cast my small shadow against your eternal skyscape.

A song for Tenzing,

Tenzing Norgay,

Surveyor of outer limits,

Sherpa,

Mountain man,

Tiger of the snows,

Because today he rests for a moment

At the top of the world,

Gazing into the bluest blue

He has ever seen!

Laughing, he embraces Hillary,

Unfurls four flags from the handle of his axe,

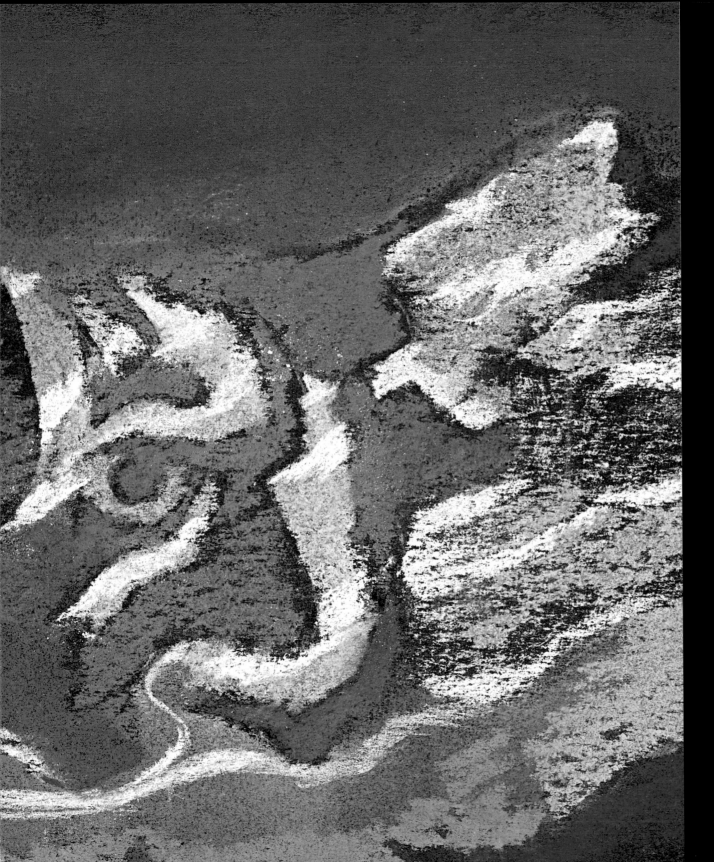

Buries his child's good-luck pencil,
Smiles into the camera's click,
Blinks in the brightness.
This moment—now—
Will not come again.

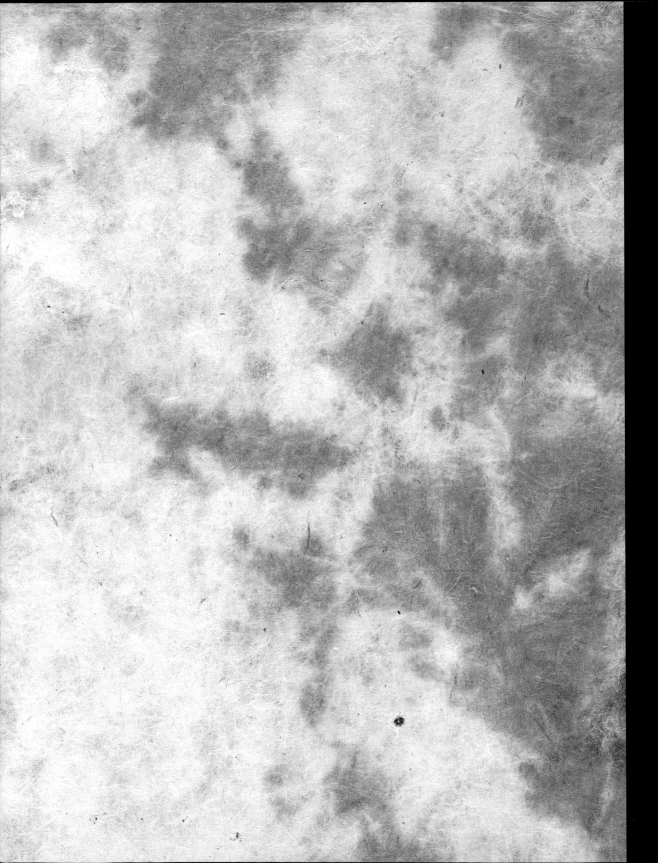

Great joy, great sadness.

He turns to go.

He must descend,

Return to the low and dreamless land,

Return to all that lies beneath this peak.

Yet something in Tenzing remains above,

Will never leave,

Stays with *his* mountain,

Joined forever to the sky:

Mountain,

Chomolungma, I am with you,

I am with you always.

AFTERWORD

On May 29, 1953, Tenzing Norgay and Edmund Hillary became the first climbers ever to reach the peak of Mt. Everest, the world's highest mountain. They stayed on the summit for just fifteen minutes! The four flags that Tenzing unfurled on the peak (though they soon blew away) were the flags of the United Nations, India, Great Britain, and Nepal.

The final day's climb of one thousand feet was the dangerous last leg of a difficult and complicated expedition. The entire team that aided Norgay and Hillary included more than three hundred carriers and fellow climbers, who together hauled seven and a half tons of supplies and equipment. The expedition started out in March and traveled through jungles to the foothills of Everest. From there, base camps were established at various heights on Everest's slopes.

Tenzing Norgay was one of the local Sherpa people who, due to their climbing skills, were and still are part of mountain-climbing teams in the Himalayas. (The Sherpas call Everest "Chomolungma.") Tenzing began his career as a carrier, and slowly, over many years, became one of the finest mountaineers in the world. Edmund Hillary was a New Zealand beekeeper with a passion for mountain climbing. Both men were chosen for the final ascent because of their experience and bravery.

Following the successful climb, both became world famous. In particular, Tenzing became a symbol of hope to millions of Asians, many of whose countries had recently gained their independence. His simple character and deep feeling for the mountains were legendary. When he died in 1986, his funeral train was nearly one mile long.

Atheneum Books for Young Readers

An imprint of Simon & Schuster Children's Publishing Division

1230 Avenue of the Americas

New York, New York 10020

Text copyright © 2006 by Robert Burleigh

Illustrations copyright © 2006 by Ed Young

Handlettering by Barbara Bash

Book design by Ann Bobco

The text for this book is set in Modula.

The illustrations for this book are rendered in pastels.

Manufactured in China

First Edition

10 9 8 7 6 5 4 3 2 1

Library of Congress Cataloging-in-Publication Data

Burleigh, Robert.

Tiger of the snows: Tenzing Norgay: the boy whose dream was Everest /

Robert Burleigh; illustrated by Ed Young.—1st ed.

p. cm.

ISBN-13: 978-0-689-83042-6

ISBN-10: 0-689-83042-4

1. Tenzing Norgay, 1914–1986. Mountaineers—India—Biography. 3. Mountaineers—Nepal—Biography.

4. Sherpa (Nepalese people)—Biography. 5. Everest, Mount (China and Nepal). I. Young, Ed, ill. II. Title.

GV199.92.T46B87 2006

796.52'2'092—dc22 2005000469